I Got a
Goldfish

Written by
David McCoy

Illustrated by
Noah Connor

I got a goldfish to play with me.
But the goldfish needed to swim.

I got a gerbil to swim with the goldfish.
But the gerbil needed to run.

I got a gorilla to run with the gerbil.
But the gorilla needed to climb.

I got a gopher to climb with the gorilla.
But the gopher needed to dig.

I got a giraffe to dig with the gopher.
But the giraffe needed to gallop.

I got a dog to gallop with the giraffe.
But the dog needed to play.

And we did.